# EXPANDING THE REPERTOIRE

# Piano Music of Black Composers

## ELEMENTARY TO UPPER EL...

Compiled and Edited by
**Leah Claiborne**

**LEVEL 1**

ISBN 978-1-70515-9-170

## HAL•LEONARD®

Visit Hal Leonard Online at
**www.halleonard.com**

World headquarters, contact:
**Hal Leonard**
7777 West Bluemound Road
Milwaukee, WI 53213
Email: info@halleonard.com

In Europe, contact:
**Hal Leonard Europe Limited**
1 Red Place
London, W1K 6PL
Email: info@halleonardeurope.com

In Australia, contact:
**Hal Leonard Australia Pty. Ltd.**
4 Lentara Court
Cheltenham, Victoria, 3192 Australia
Email: info@halleonard.com.au

# Foreword

For far too long, the contributions of Black composers in the piano repertoire have not been brought to the forefront. Despite a persistent wave of great scholarship to bring awareness of these composers to light, only recently has there been deliberate inclusion of their works. Even with more awareness and attempts for inclusion, the myth that there is only piano music by Black composers for advanced pianists remains. We often look at great composers as solely creators of advanced repertoire, but we forget that many of them specifically wrote music for their own students of all skill levels. Finally there is a pedagogical piano collection that celebrates Black composers as pedagogues and gathers together piano music that can be enjoyed by the most novice beginning piano student through their musical progress.

Having this music available at the most fundamental levels of a student's development sets the tone for what can and should be expected as the student progresses. When teachers introduce Black composers at the earliest stages of study, the student will not be surprised to be learning a piece by a Black composer later when they are more advanced. On the contrary, students and teachers will begin to learn, discover, and greatly appreciate the pedagogical benefits of incorporating this music into the teaching repertoire at all stages and levels of learning.

Each piece in this collection was specifically chosen to help address some of the most fundamental musical and technical challenges that young pianists encounter. A student who is currently in a primer or early beginning method book would be able to use these wonderful pieces to help reinforce many concepts. Both books are in progressive order, so that representation by Black composers is available to them throughout their musical journey.

The music in Book 1 showcases a wide range of character, style periods, and musical concepts for the young pianist. For example, the first piece in the series not only shows the pianist how to build a beautiful melody with the left hand, but also how to pass the thumb in a musical way. This study for the left hand alone has basic notation on the staff, suitable for students who are just becoming more familiar with notation. Books 1 and 2 both include selections from Blanche K. Thomas' "Plantation Songs in Easy Arrangements." Thomas stressed and advocated for the inclusion of Negro Spirituals in musical curriculum and to utilize these melodies in various ways for learning. The intentional inclusion of these Spirituals, with the lyrics, allows students to gain understanding of culture, history, rhythmic complexities, and phrase structures at an appropriate level for early beginners.

The pieces in these books not only celebrate Black composers but also aim to celebrate diverse student populations studying classical piano music. When students see themselves represented in the music that they study, it encourages and normalizes their own musical pursuit. With such a wide variety of music spanning over two hundred years, students and teachers will gain great appreciation and enjoy learning these piano works by Black composers for beginning pianists.

—Leah Claiborne, editor

# Contents

*Music is laid out in progressive order. Fingerings are editorial additions.*

# Pedagogical Notes

### Left Alone by Leah Claiborne

This piece allows the young pianist to develop a cantabile melody with only using the left hand, and to pass the thumb effectively under the hand to create a balanced and smooth melodic line.

### Jumping the Broom by Leah Claiborne

"Jumping the Broom" is a practice in many African-American weddings which was passed down from the enslaved. At the end of the ceremony, the groom and bride face their guests, hold hands, and jump over a broom, solidifying their union. The pianist can solidify their understanding of the two note slurs that occur in both hands. The repeated C's should remain soft as if a distant drum in the background.

### Chit-Chat by Leah Claiborne

This fun and jazz-like melody is full of pedagogical bundles for musical development. The pianist should pay close attention to the various articulation markings in each hand to portray a conversation happening between the hands. At the repeat, the pianist can add their own creative articulations/conversations at the piano!

### The King's Magic Drum by Leah Claiborne

This popular folk story tells a tale of a king who used his drum to create an enchanting atmosphere over his enemies. When the drum would be played, a great feast of food, dance, and fun would come over the land, making his enemies forget about any discontentment. The pianist will develop a strong hand position as they play the repeated fifth intervals, signifying the drums. The right hand is asked to handle various articulations that bring the story to life!

### Slumber Song by Ulysses Kay

This dreamy piece of music is full of wonderful musical elements to help the young pianist develop many technical skills. Both hands are challenged to handle two-note slurs in various intervals and fingerings, and they both contribute to the soft and sleepy melody. Careful attention should be given to the pedal. Although the pedaling remains the same for most of the piece, encourage the pianist to listen to the sound quality they are creating at the piano. Experiment with using quarter, half, or full pedal to train the ear and foot to work together.

### The Unsung by Leah Claiborne

This is a wonderful piece to help a student play a long melodic line in the right hand while also handling broken chord passage work for the left hand. The left hand can be practiced by blocking the chords to allow more attention on the right-hand melody. Singing the melody will also help the student to feel the long held melodic notes. Careful attention should be made to voice the melodic notes shared by left hand and right hand at mm. 16 and 17. This sad tune is in remembrance of all those who lost their life to their oppressors.

### Go Down, Moses (arr. Blanche K. Thomas)

"Go Down, Moses" is a popular melody set in a harmonic minor key. Careful attention should be given to help create a legato left hand which can be achieved with attention to the fingering of the left hand. In many spirituals, the "weak" beat is emphasized. Can you find moments in the music where beat two is emphasized? This allows for the words to guide our musicality. The composer encourages the young pianist to sing the words as they practice to help with their understanding of phrase structures.

### I'm Troubled in Mind (arr. Blanche K. Thomas)

"I'm Troubled in Mind" is a beautiful yet sorrowful spiritual. Blanche Thomas sets the tune in a brief imitation which allows the young pianist to develop coordination in a unique and pedagogically fruitful way. Following the lyrics will help guide the pianist's ear for handling the melody in both hands. Short imitative moments form a great predecessor for the foundation of contrapuntal music like inventions, sinfonias, and fugues. The composer also writes, "This tune may be used as an example of the use of the pure minor scale. Call attention to the absence of the raised 7th tone of the scale, either ascending or descending." The melody in the right hand in the second part is imitated for two measures.

### Lift Every Voice and Sing by James & John Johnson, arr. Leah Claiborne

"Lift Every Voice and Sing" is a song of unity, pride, and liberation. The words and music were composed by brothers James Weldon Johnson and John Rosamond Johnson for the 91st anniversary of Abraham Lincoln's birthday. Today, many people consider this song to be the Black National Anthem. It is often customary for people to stand when this piece is being sung and performed. This particular arrangement fits comfortably in the hands for the young pianist. Careful attention should be used in the left-hand intervals to voice to the top note to keep a balanced sonority. Practice balancing the treble and bass register of the piano when the hands are in unison. A steady, calm wrist will allow for even tones when the hands play continuous eighth notes, especially when moving from black to white keys.

### We Are Climbing Jacob's Ladder (arr. Blanche K. Thomas)

The composer highlights that the rhythm in the first measure, which is continuously repeated throughout the piece, should be isolated and understood. The pianist should aim to voice the melodic notes starting at m. 5. This is a wonderful exercise for developing voicing in both hands for a well-balanced performance.

### Steal Away (arr. Blanche K. Thomas)

"Steal Away" is a Spiritual that is considered to be a code song, which the enslaved sang to one another to communicate hidden messages on how to escape from slavery. "Steal Away" utilizes the dotted quarter followed by an eighth note rhythm throughout the piece which can be a challenge for young pianist. The composer encourages the pianist to develop this rhythmic pattern by isolating four specific measures: mm 1, 9, 11, 13.

### Tryin' to Make Heaven My Home (arr. Blanche K. Thomas)

This encouraging song has a message of perseverance! The repeated notes should be shaped in the melody and careful attention should be given to the two note slurs in the right hand.

### Lord, I Want to Be a Christian (arr. Blanche K. Thomas)

This intimate and simple melody allows the pianist to develop great musical sensitivity in their playing. The pianist should pay close attention to the many dynamic and tempo changes which are the composer's own markings. This will allow for a convincing and musical performance. The composer also highlights m. 2 as a potential rhythmic problem that should be isolated and understood.

### Lady Mary Montague's Reel by Ignatius Sancho

This is a wonderful pedagogical piece that many pianists enjoy performing. Ignatius Sancho wrote out dance movements for each piece which is a reminder that this music was composed for social and entertaining purposes! Encourage students to use their imagination to create fitting dance movements to go along with this piece, a great way to get excited about music in the early classical style.

This piece gives students experience with wide quarter note leaps in the left hand and running eighth note passages in the right hand. The music is a blank canvas for creativity and can help foster many musical elements such as incorporating ornamentations at the repeats. Consider using this piece alongside or in addition to Gavotte in G Major, HWV 491 by Handel which utilizes many of the same pedagogical elements.

## An Asphodel for Marcel by Hale Smith

The repetition of the left hand not only helps to solidify a solid hand position, but also allows for the pianist to focus their attention on handling this beautiful relaxing melody. The right hand should aim to create even notes when playing the eighth notes in the opening. Careful voicing attention should be given to the right-hand chords.

## Blooz by Hale Smith

The composer writes: "The repeated notes in the right hand are to be played as a quietly blurred background which surrounds the melody much as a forest surrounds a landscape." This beautiful imagery will help the pianist to create a light touch with the right hand to allow the melody to shine through. This can be accomplished by keeping the right hand relaxed and taking the weight out of the hand. Experiment with how much weight is needed on the keys. Each piano is different and will require the pianist to adjust to the sound that the piano is producing. The composer also writes: "The pedal should be used carefully throughout to create a harmonic haze, but the melody should never be obscured by over-pedaling." This piece can be used alongside Cornelius Gurlitt's Etude in D minor, Op. 82, No. 65, which teaches many of the same topics.

# Left Alone

Leah Claiborne

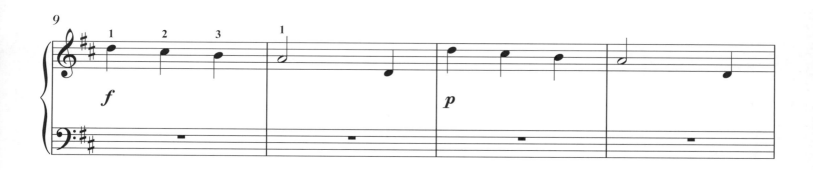

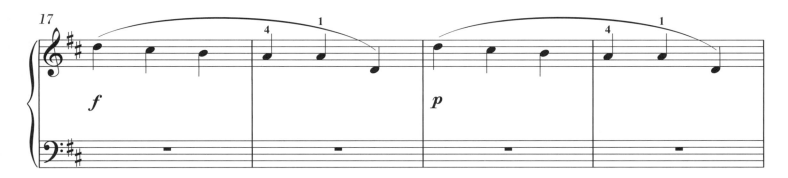

# Jumping the Broom

Leah Claiborne

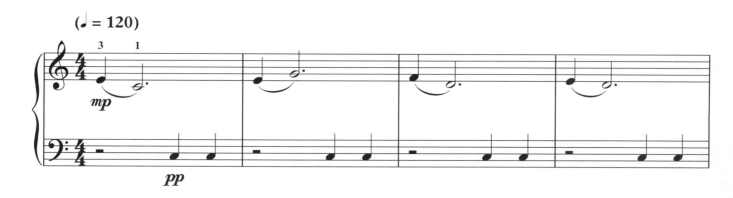

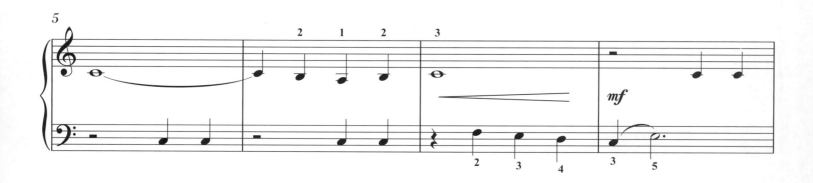

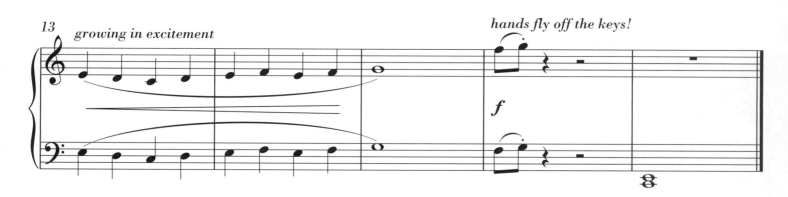

# Chit-Chat

Leah Claiborne

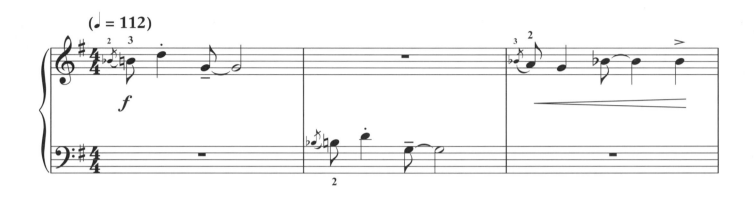

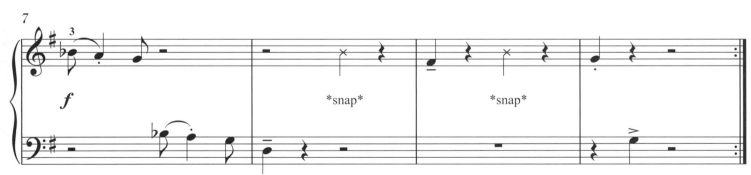

*At the repeat, student should create*
*their own articulations & dynamics!*

# The King's Magic Drum

Leah Claiborne

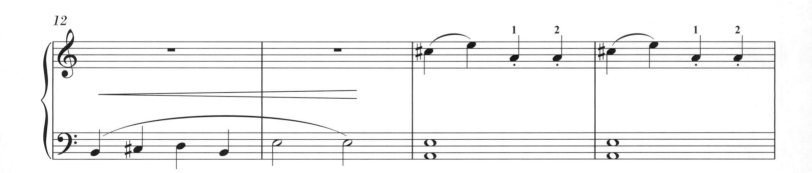

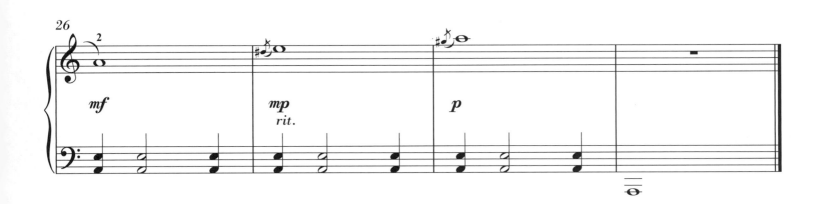

# Slumber Song
## from 10 SHORT ESSAYS FOR PIANO

Ulysses Kay

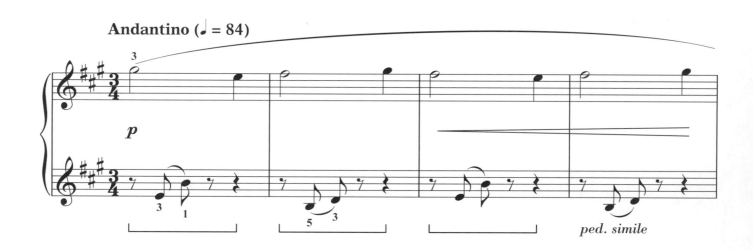

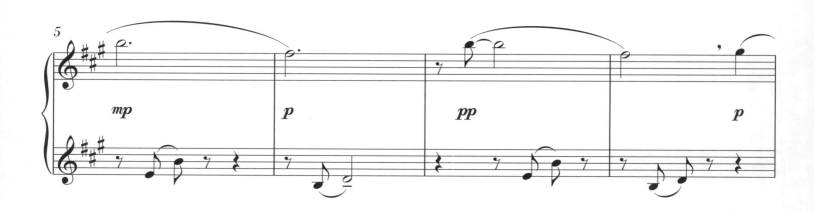

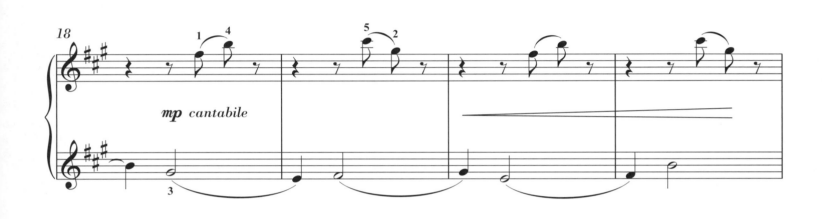

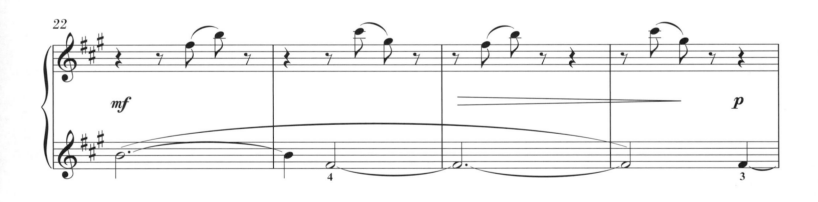

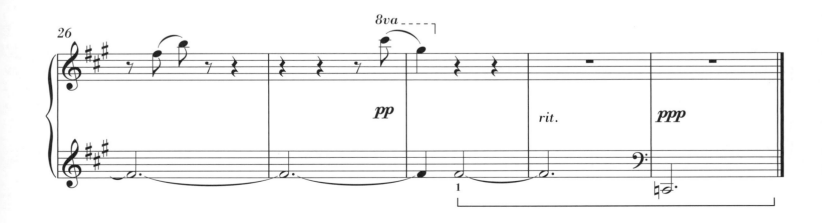

# The Unsung

Leah Claiborne

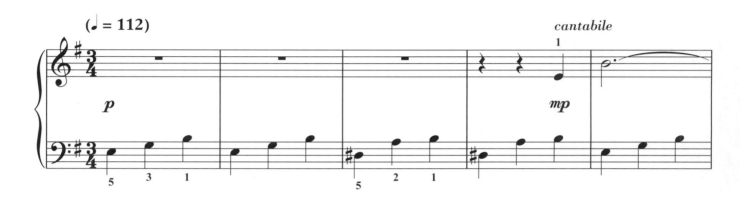

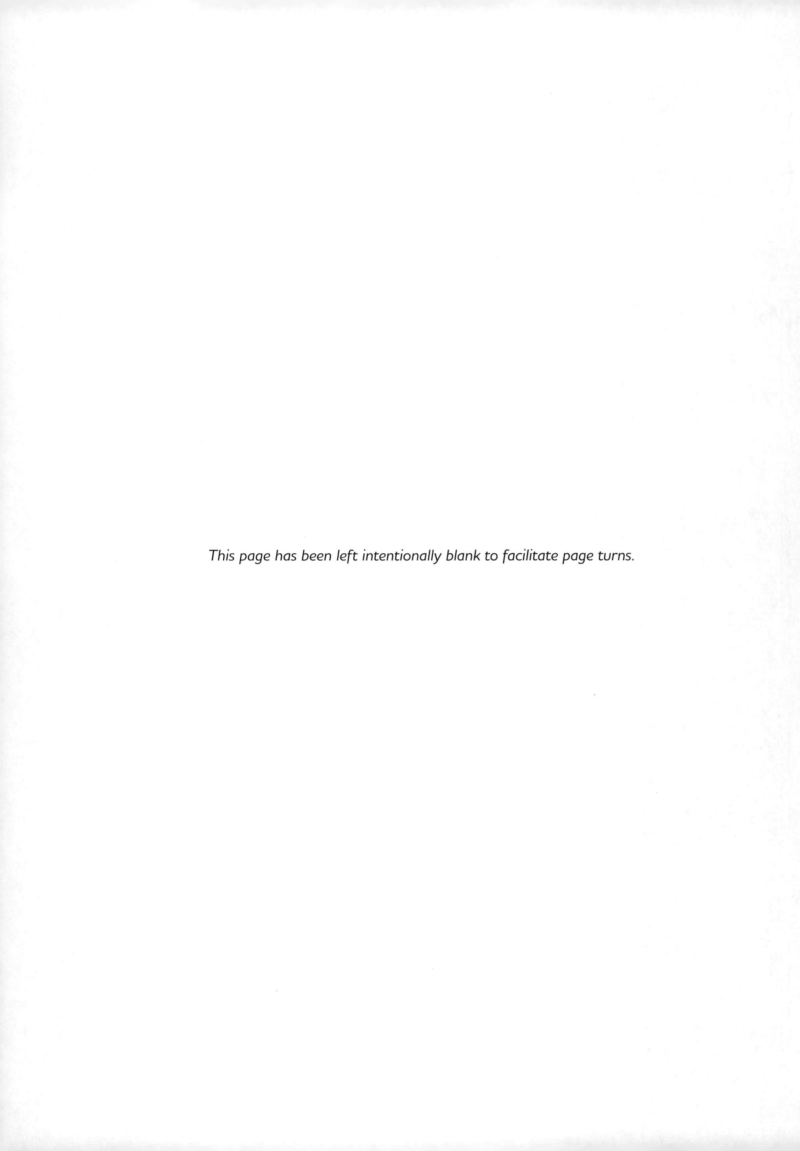

*This page has been left intentionally blank to facilitate page turns.*

# Go Down, Moses
## from PLANTATION SONGS IN EASY ARRANGEMENTS

Traditional African-American Spiritual
Arranged by Blanche K. Thomas

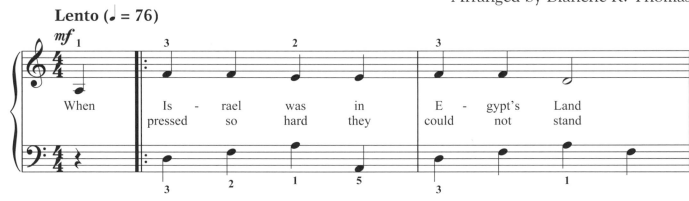

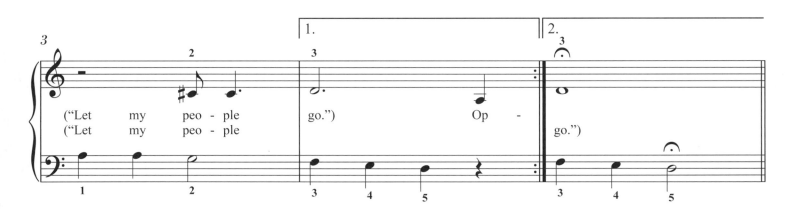

When Is - rael was in E - gypt's Land
pressed so hard in they could not Land stand

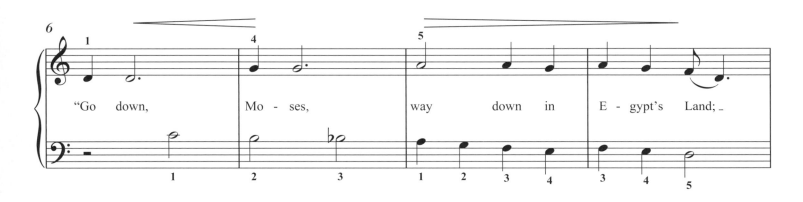

("Let my peo - ple go.") Op -
("Let my peo - ple go.")

"Go down, Mo - ses, way down in E - gypt's Land;

Tell old Pha - raoh to let my peo - ple go."

# I'm Troubled in Mind
## from PLANTATION SONGS IN EASY ARRANGEMENTS

Traditional African-American Spiritual
Arranged by Blanche K. Thomas

*It is said that after a slave had been whipped,*
*he would sing this song.*

*Refrain:*
I'm troubled, I'm troubled, I'm troubled in mind;
If Jesus don't help me, I surely will die.

O Jesus, my Saviour, on thee I depend;
When troubles are near me, you'll be my true friend.
*Refrain*

Je - sus my \_\_\_ Sav - iour, on Thee I de - pend; When

troub - les are \_\_ near me, you'll be \_\_ my true friend. I'm

troub - led, I'm \_\_ troub - led, I'm troub - led in \_\_ mind; If

Je - sus don't \_ help me, I sure - ly will die.

# Lift Every Voice and Sing

Words and Music by James Weldon Johnson
and J. Rosamond Johnson
Arranged by Leah Claiborne

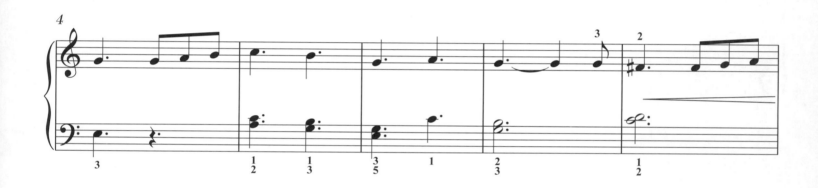

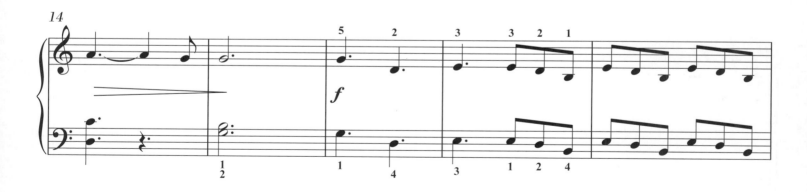

Lift every voice and sing
Till earth and heaven ring,
Ring with the harmonies of Liberty;
Let our rejoicing rise
High as the listening skies,
Let it resound loud as the rolling sea.
Sing a song full of the faith that the dark past has taught us,
Sing a song full of the hope that the present has brought us,
Facing the rising sun of our new day begun
Let us march on till victory is won.

Stony the road we trod,
Bitter the chastening rod,
Felt in the days when hope unborn had died;
Yet with a steady beat,
Have not our weary feet
Come to the place for which our fathers sighed?
We have come over a way that with tears has been watered,
We have come, treading our path through the blood of the slaughtered,
Out from the gloomy past,
Till now we stand at last
Where the white gleam of our bright star is cast.

God of our weary years,
God of our silent tears,
Thou who has brought us thus far on the way;
Thou who has by Thy might Led us into the light,
Keep us forever in the path, we pray.
Lest our feet stray from the places, our God, where we met Thee,
Lest, our hearts drunk with the wine of the world, we forget Thee;
Shadowed beneath Thy hand,
May we forever stand.
True to our God,
True to our native land.

# We Are Climbing Jacob's Ladder

## from PLANTATION SONGS IN EASY ARRANGEMENTS

Traditional African-American Spiritual
Arranged by Blanche K. Thomas

**Trionfante (♩ = 120)**

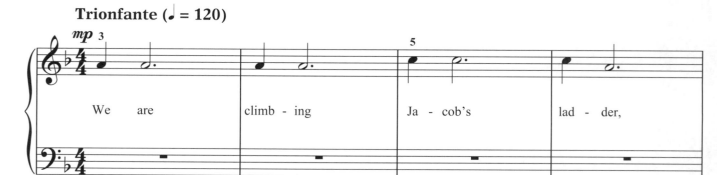

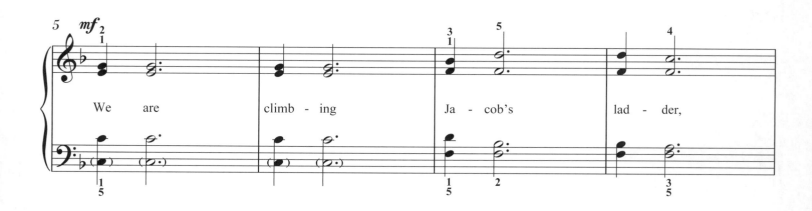

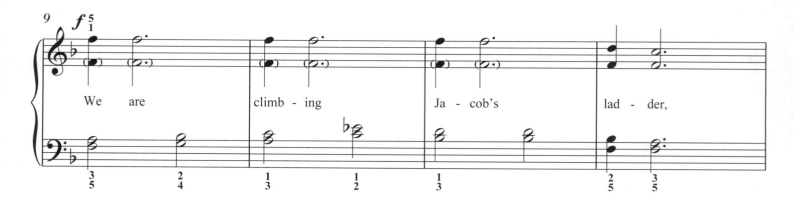

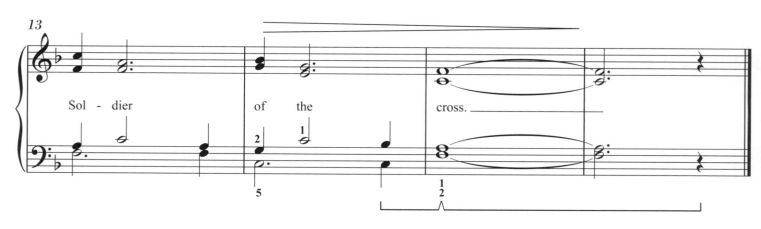

# Steal Away
## from PLANTATION SONGS IN EASY ARRANGEMENTS

Traditional African-American Spiritual
Arranged by Blanche K. Thomas

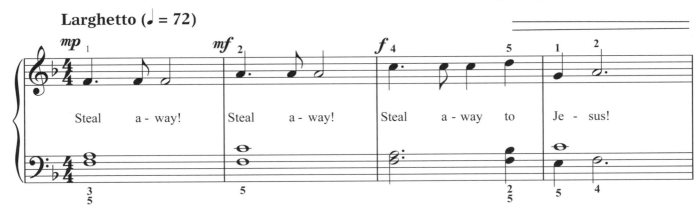

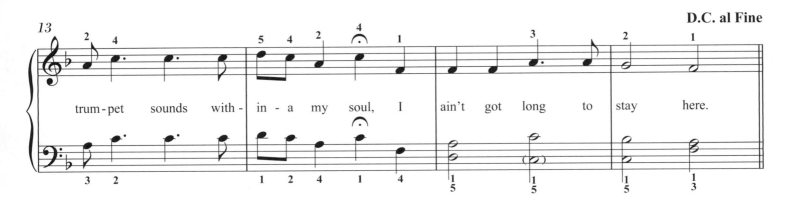

# Tryin' to Make Heaven My Home
## from PLANTATION SONGS IN EASY ARRANGEMENTS

Traditional African-American Spiritual
Arranged by Blanche K. Thomas

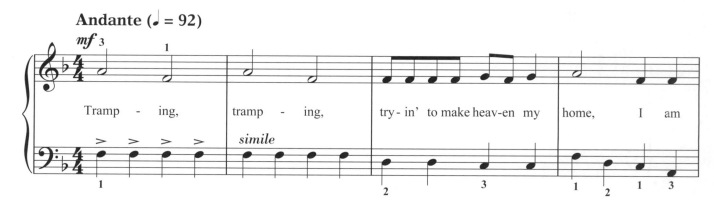

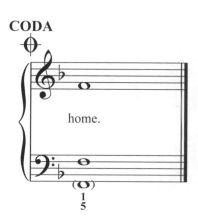

# Lord, I Want to Be a Christian
## from PLANTATION SONGS IN EASY ARRANGEMENTS

Traditional African-American Spiritual
Arranged by Blanche K. Thomas

# Lady Mary Montague's Reel
## from 12 COUNTRY DANCES FOR THE YEAR 1779

Ignatius Sancho

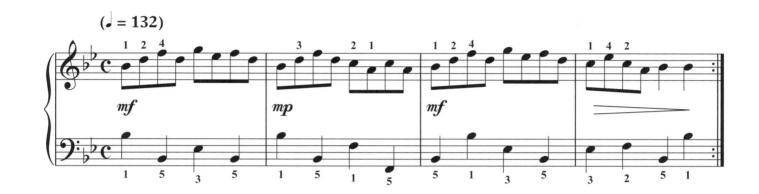

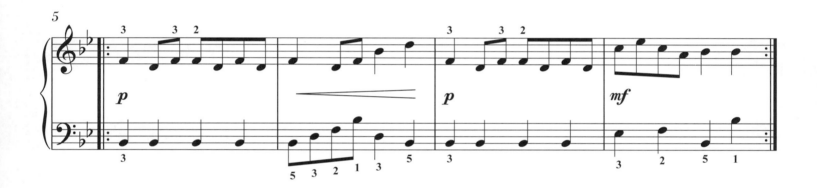

# An Asphodel for Marcel
## from FACES OF JAZZ

Hale Smith

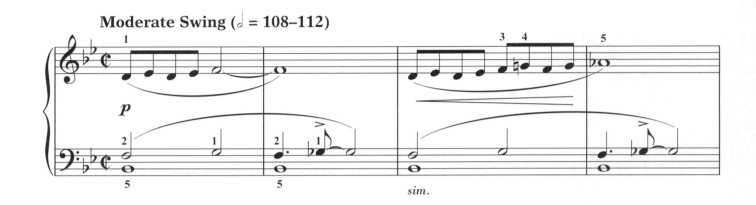

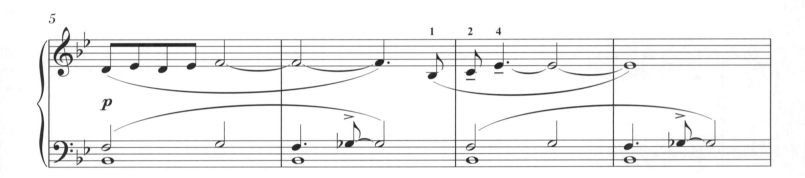

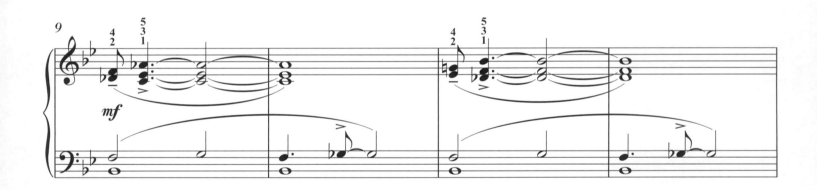

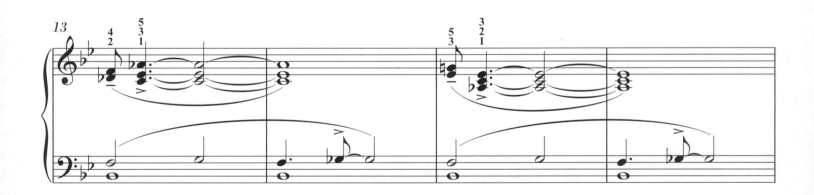

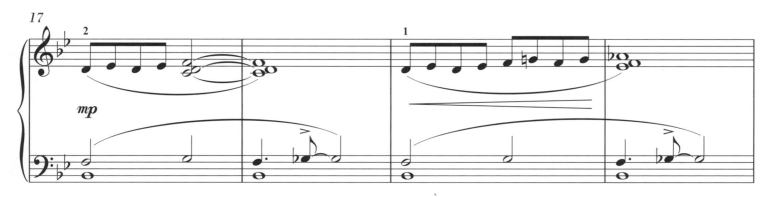

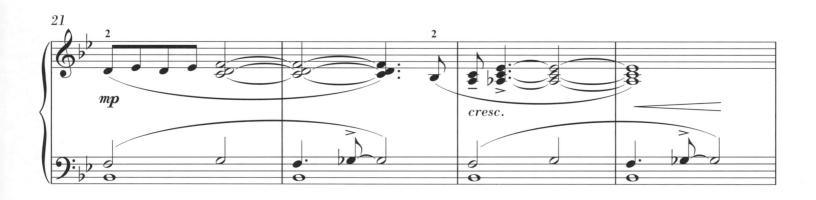

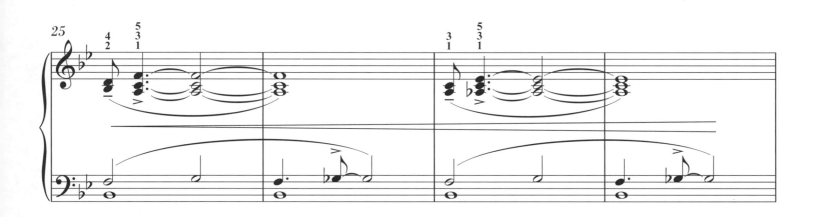

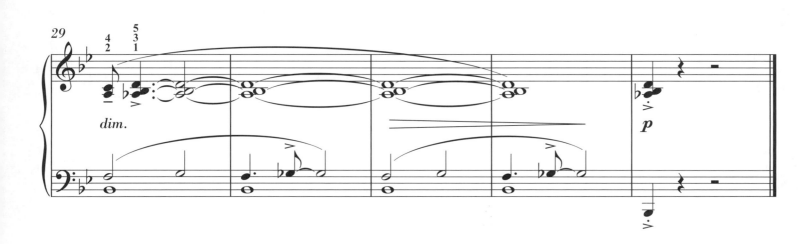

*for Ahmad Jamal*

# Blooz
## from FACES OF JAZZ

Hale Smith

*The pedal should be used carefully throughout to create a harmonic haze, but the melody should never be obscured by over-pedaling.